THE BEST OF
AUDRA McDONALD

ISBN 978-1-4584-1982-8

HAL•LEONARD®
CORPORATION
7777 W. BLUEMOUND RD. P.O. BOX 13819 MILWAUKEE, WI 53213

Visit Hal Leonard Online at
www.halleonard.com

CONTENTS

ANY PLACE I HANG MY HAT IS HOME

Words by JOHNNY MERCER
Music by HAROLD ARLEN

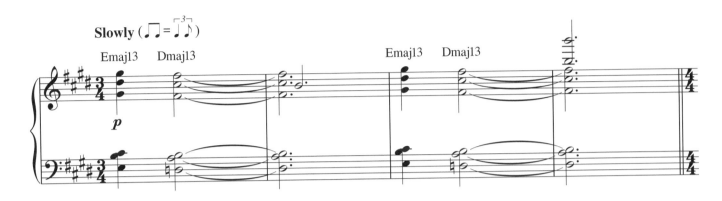

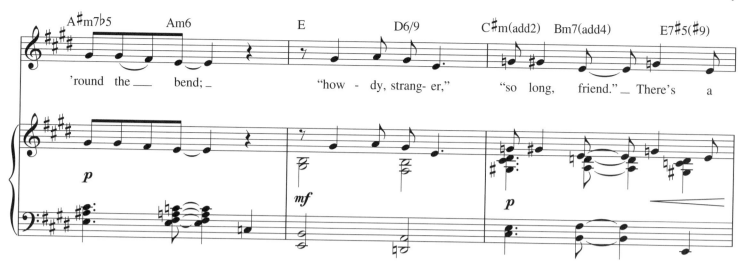

'round the ___ bend; _ "how - dy, strang- er," "so long, friend." _ There's a

voice in the lone - some wind ___ that keeps whis-per - in', ___ "Roam," ___

___ 'cause an - y - place I hang my hat is home.

AS TIME GOES BY

Words and Music by
HERMAN HUPFELD

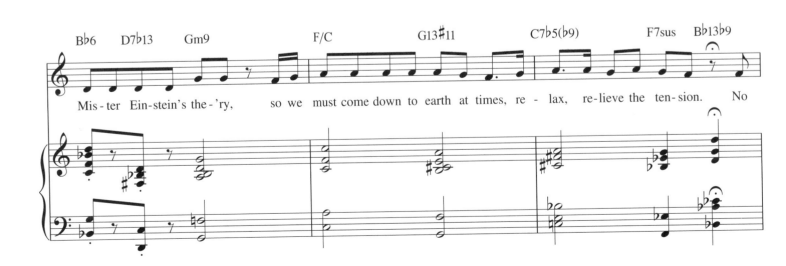

BABY MOON

Music and Lyrics by
ADAM GUETTEL

Curled up in - side of me... I feel_____ you. Like a

warm ball of light wait - ing for_____ dawn._____

blow. The last thing I want is to shock or up-

- set you. I have-n't e-ven met you. But

you've got to know!

My ba - by moon …

poco rit.   a tempo

I'm no he - ro. I'm not wise.

Not like the moth - ers I see.

I don't know an - y lul - la - bies.

(brighter mood)

But I'm a sing - er and I can sing to ya the sound of what you mean

HOW GLORY GOES

from FLOYD COLLINS

Music and Lyrics by
ADAM GUETTEL

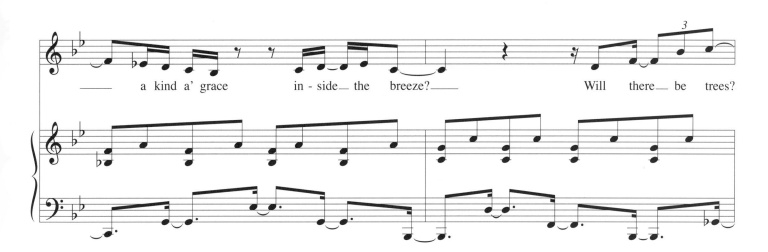

Will I want, Will I wish____ for all____ the things____

____ I should have done, Long - ing to fin - ish what____ I on -

- ly just____ be - gun?____ Or has a shin - in' truth been wait - in' there____ for

8vb ____   *loco*

all the ques - tions ev - 'ry - where? In a world a' wond - 'rin', sud - den - ly you

BUILD A BRIDGE

from MYTHS AND HYMNS

Music and Lyrics by
ADAM GUETTEL

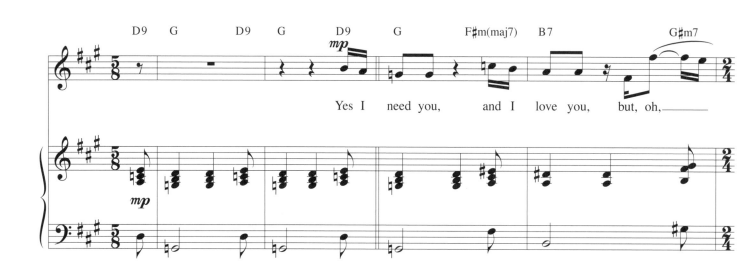

Yes I need you, and I love you, but, oh,_____

_____ the wa-ter's wide..._____ Oh, yes. I am try-ing. I am__

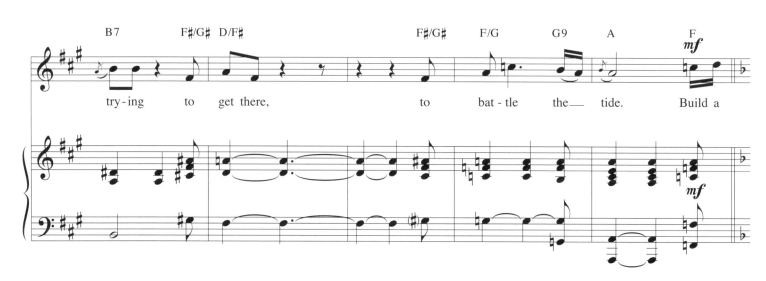

try-ing to get there, to bat-tle the__ tide. Build a

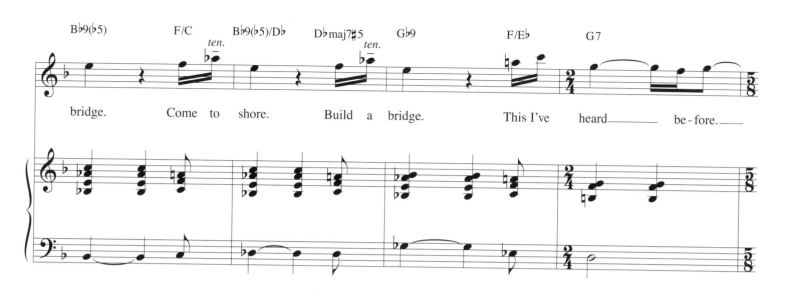

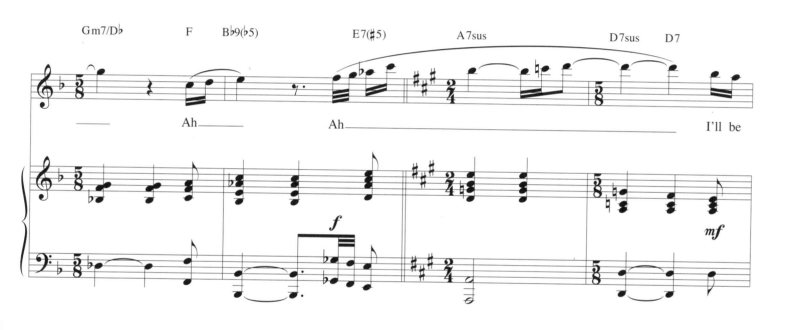

need you, and I love you, but, oh,_____ the wa-ter's wide._____ Oh, yes. I am

try-ing. I am try-ing to get there, to bat-tle the_ tide.

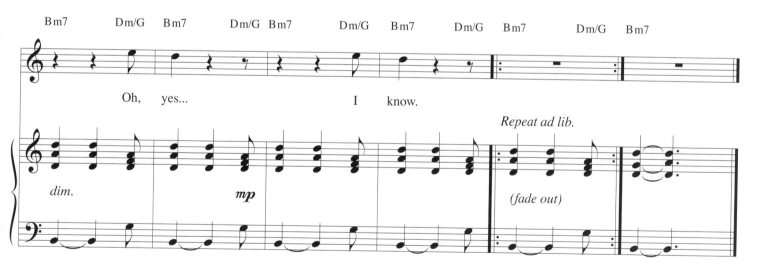

Oh, yes... I know.

dim. *mp* *(fade out)*

Repeat ad lib.

CRADLE AND ALL

Music by RICKY IAN GORDON
Lyrics by JESSICA MOLASKEY
with RICKY IAN GORDON

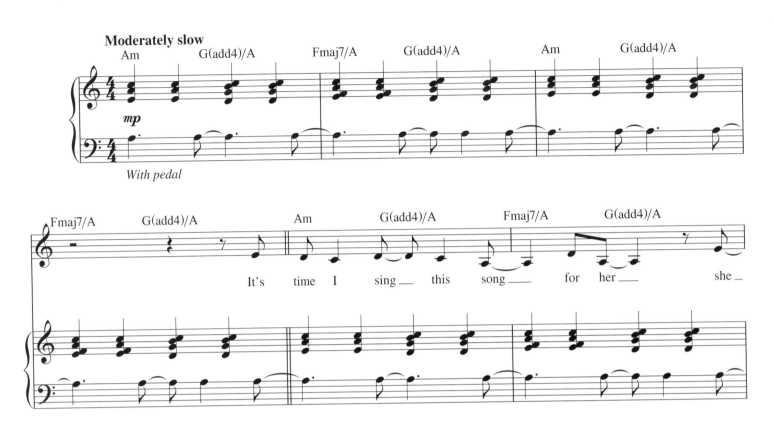

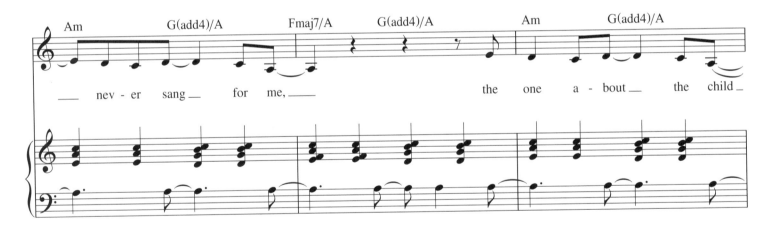

It's time I sing ___ this song ___ for her ___ she ___ nev-er sang ___ for me, ___ the one a-bout ___ the child ___

___ fall - ing from ___ the fam - 'ly tree. ___ It's

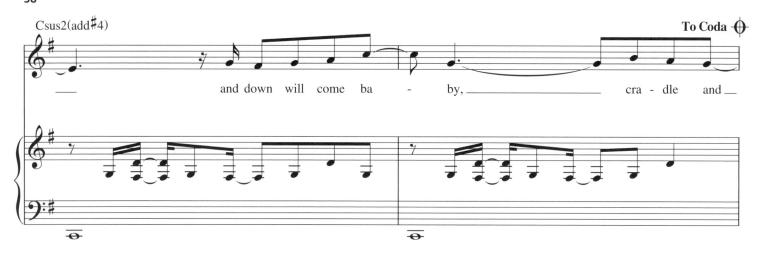

To Coda ⊕

and down will come ba - by, _____ cra - dle and ____

____ all. _____

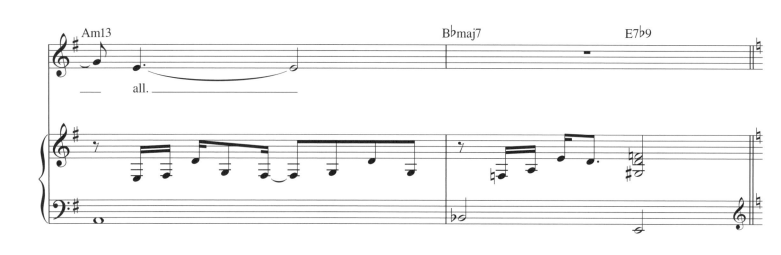

It's time I wrote ___ that song ___ for him ___ he ___

I DOUBLE DARE YOU

Words and Music by TERRY SHAND
and JIMMY EATON

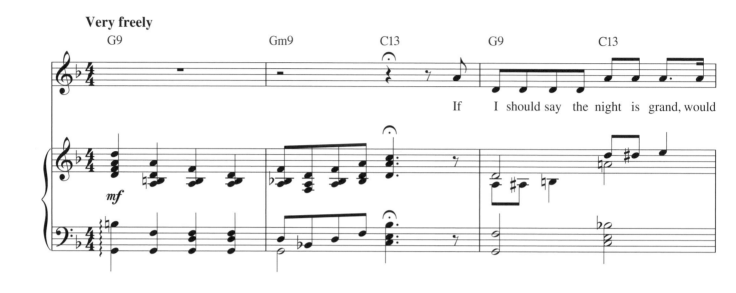

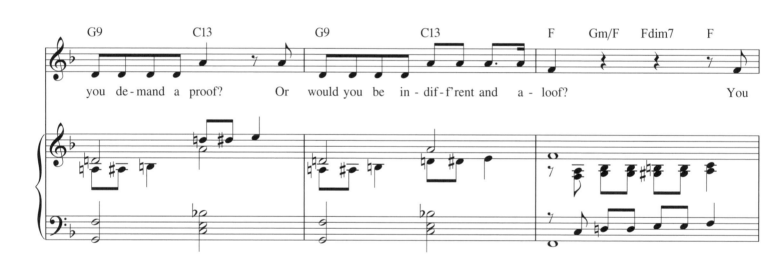

I FOLLOW

Music and Lyrics by
JENNY GIERING

Slowly, softly, and very, very freely

Some-one some-where is laugh-ing. Some-one some-where sings a sor-ry lit-tle song. Some-one some-where is call-ing me, And I fol-low. For the

feed this_____ dis - tance,_____ When I_____ fol - low._____

For the si - lence of____ my____ mind is deaf - en - ing.

Come and find me_____ here._____ Ah...

Ah..._____

Ah..._____

(both)

Ah...

Ah...

Ah...

(I) Wear your love___ like_ a

shoe - string. (II) Wear your heart ex - posed and un - a -

ware. (I) Wear a prom-ise— so it calls———— me,——— (II) And I— fol-low.——

(I) For the si-lence of—— my— mind is deaf-en-ing. *(both)* Come and find me——

—— here.—— Ah...——————— Ah...———

Ah...—————————

Ah…

Ah…

Ah…

Ah…

Ah…

Ah…

Ah…

Ah…

Ah…

I HID MY LOVE

By STEVE MARZULLO
Poem by JOHN CLARE

hid my love when young till I could-n't bear the buz - zing of a fly. I

hid my love to my de-spite till I could not bear to look at light; I

dare not gaze up - on her face but left her mem - 'ry in each place; Where-

ev - er I saw a wild flower lie I kissed and bade my love Good-

bye. I

met her in the green - est dells, Where dew - drops pearl the wood blue bells; The

lost breeze kissed— her bright blue eye The bee kissed and went sing - ing by, A

poco accel.

sun - beam found a pass - age there A gold chain round her neck so fair, As

se - cret as the wild bee's song She lay there all the sum - mer

a tempo   *poco accel.*   *poco rall.*

long.⎯⎯⎯⎯⎯⎯⎯⎯⎯⎯⎯⎯⎯⎯⎯⎯⎯⎯   I

Con poco moto

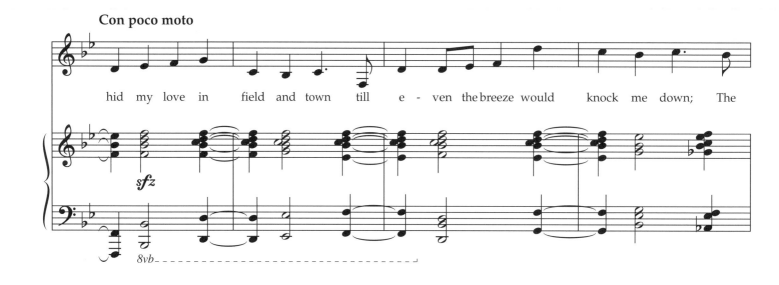

hid my love in field and town till e - ven the breeze would knock me down; The

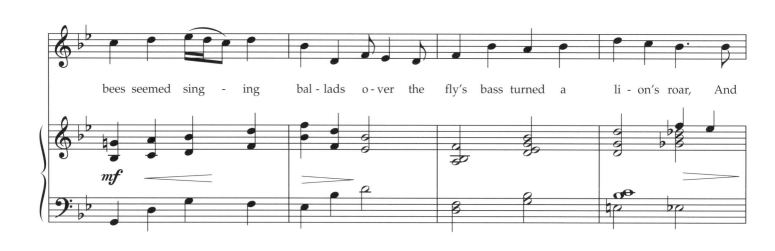

bees seemed sing - ing bal - lads o - ver the fly's bass turned a li - on's roar, And

e - ven si - lence found a tongue to haunt me all the sum - mer long; The

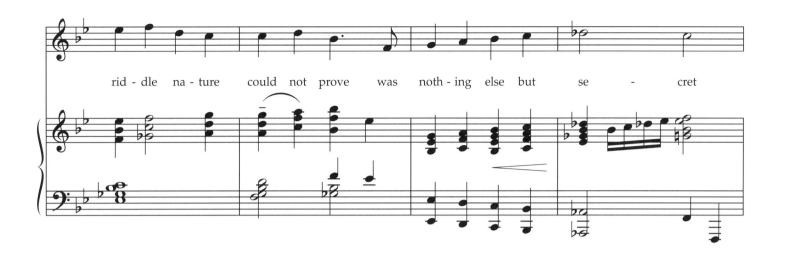

rid - dle na - ture could not prove was noth - ing else but se - cret

love, Was noth - ing else but se - cret

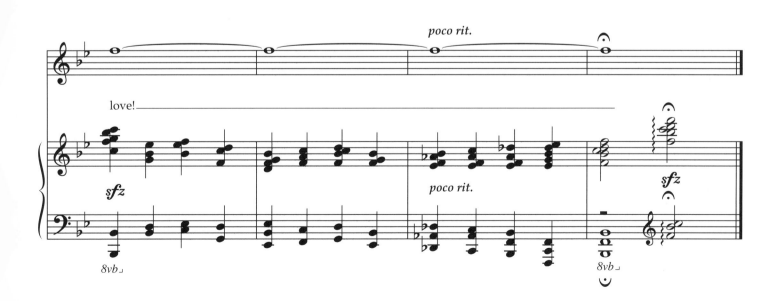

love!

I THINK IT'S GOING TO RAIN TODAY

Words and Music by
RANDY NEWMAN

IS IT REALLY ME?
from 110 IN THE SHADE

Words by TOM JONES
Music by HARVEY SCHMIDT

I WANNA GET MARRIED

Words and Music by
NELLIE McKAY

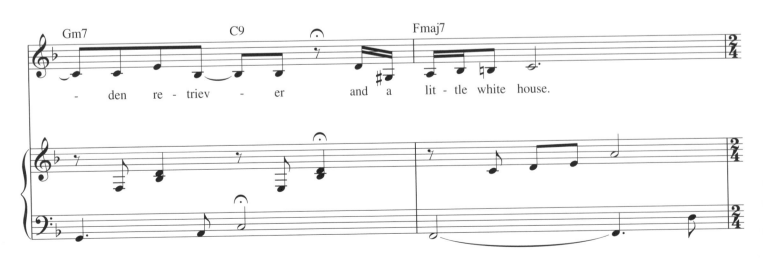

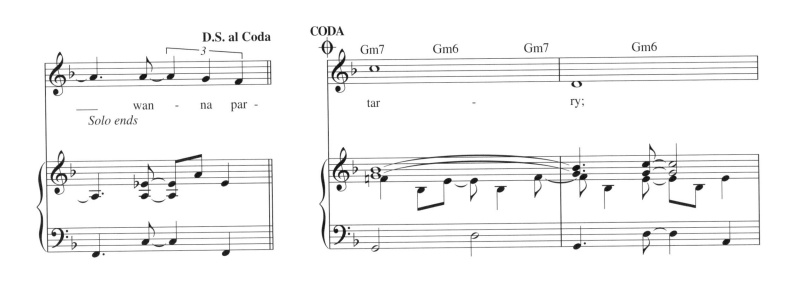

A LITTLE BIT IN LOVE

from WONDERFUL TOWN

Music by LEONARD BERNSTEIN
Lyrics by BETTY COMDEN
and ADOLPH GREEN

THE MAN THAT GOT AWAY

Lyric by IRA GERSHWIN
Music by HAROLD ARLEN

SEE WHAT I WANNA SEE

Words and Music by
JOHN La CHIUSA

*L.H. pitched as written or played percussively through measure 8.

ev - 'ry - one was do - in' the lim - bo ex - cept for

Sal - ly and her Po - dunk plug.____ Seems____

____ he took a shine to some chick - en,

shak - in' her tom - tom - tom; Sal - ly saw that____ and Gua-

ca - mole!* She ex - plod - ed like the hy - dro - gen bomb!__

__ She cried:__ "Hey, hey!__ What-cha do - in'? What-cha do - in'?__ What's she__

palms gliss. on white keys

__ got that I lack?__ That chick - en is thin__ and mean-

er than sin____ and ug - li - er than Bam - boo

*sung as one syllable

96

STARS AND THE MOON

from SONGS FOR A NEW WORLD

Music and Lyrics by
JASON ROBERT BROWN

SUPPER TIME

from the Stage Production AS THOUSANDS CHEER

Words and Music by
IRVING BERLIN

TELL ME

from MARIE CHRISTINE

Words and Music by
JOHN La CHIUSA

love, _____ if for all I gave to you your ar - ro - gance is

all you have to show. I'll be the fear of a fire at sea. _____

I'll be the sound of a com - ing storm. _____

I'll take a - way what you think is yours. _____

I'll take a - way what I gave to you. _____ You don't

know how far _____ I'd go. _____

TESS'S TORCH SONG

Music by HAROLD ARLEN
Words by TED KOEHLER

WHEN DID I FALL IN LOVE

from the Musical FIORELLO!

Words by SHELDON HARNICK
Music by JERRY BOCK

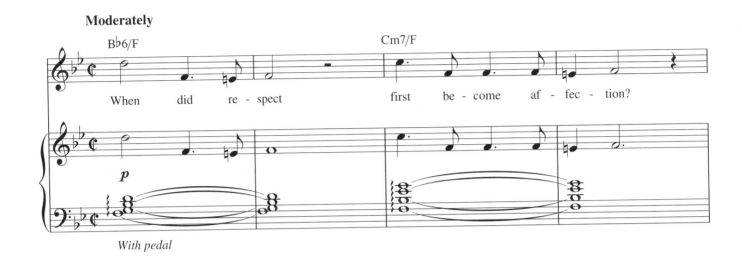

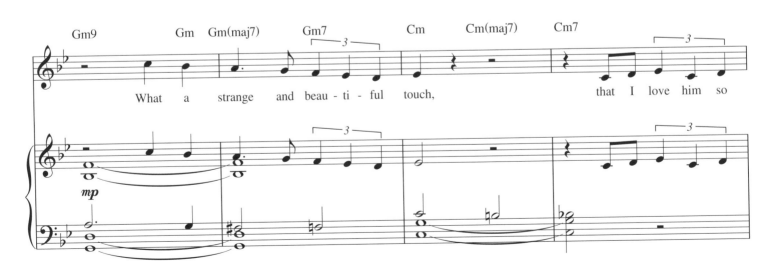

YOU DON'T KNOW THIS MAN
from PARADE

Music and Lyrics by
JASON ROBERT BROWN

Arranged for this folio by the composer

And you don't know...

Tempo primo

And you___ nev-er will. Not from me, not from

an-y-one who knows him, Not a mor-sel, not a crumb, not a clue.

(freely)

I have noth-ing more to say to you.

YOUR DADDY'S SON
from RAGTIME

Lyrics by LYNN AHRENS
Music by STEPHEN FLAHERTY